Embroidery Machine
ESSENTIALS
Piecing Techniques

By Jeanine Twigg

©2006 Jeanine Twigg

Published by

700 East State Street • Iola, WI 54990-0001
715-445-2214 • 888-457-2873

Our toll-free number to place an order or obtain a free catalog is (800) 258-0929.

Embroidery Design Copyright Information

Library of Congress Catalog Number: 2006921921

ISBN-13: 978-0-89689-142-5

ISBN-10: 0-89689-142-9

Edited by Maria L. Turner

Designed by Emily Adler

Printed in China

Table of Contents

Introduction

This book was perhaps the most fun of all to create. The possibilities of foundation piecing on a sewing machine and an embroidery machine are endless!

There are so many traditional quilt blocks that can be foundation-pieced. It was tough to limit my choices to only 20! So, I created embroidery designs to fit five categories: Sewing Machine Piecing, Basic Embroidery Machine Piecing, Crazy Piecing, Applipiecing (combining appliqué techniques with piecing) and Creative Piecing. Each technique throughout the book moves you toward my favorite—Creative Piecing—which combines all the techniques into one fun-filled piecing extravaganza.

There are never enough hours in a day to explore all the options one embroidery design can offer. I was still piecing long after turning in the manuscript to the publisher. Once you get going, you just can't stop!

No matter if you have a sewing machine or embroidery machine, each pattern or design on the enclosed CD has an infinite number of possible variations. A single design can look completely different, depending on the fabrics and combinations you choose. I loved experimenting with fabric color, but the quilt fabric manufacturers do not make the selection process easy! They produce some of the most gorgeous fabrics in the world. From fat quarters to die-cut 5" to 10" squares, rely on your local quilt fabric store to color-coordinate fabric assortments for you. This makes the piecing process so much easier. Simply take each square, fat-eighth or fat-quarter in the order prepared by the quilt shop, cut fabric strips the width(s) needed for the design and piece away. Many of the patterns or designs travel by segment around in a circle, such as crazy patch or log cabin blocks. Start with the first color and continue piecing one color to the next. Once you've reached the end of the block, start over no matter where you are in the fabric pile. No two blocks are the same and the finished creations explode with color. You'll be hooked!

In addition to the piecing designs on the CD, I've included an assortment of quilting designs to hold your project layers together. Most of the designs can be used alone or in conjunction with the piecing designs to create even more possibilities. The tiny designs are created no larger than 1½" square to fit into the centers of some blocks. Check out the black-and-white projects; these are some of my favorites and they include some of the tiny embroidery designs.

Enjoy discovering the fun behind these creative techniques. Trust me: Once you start, you can't stitch just one!

Jeanine

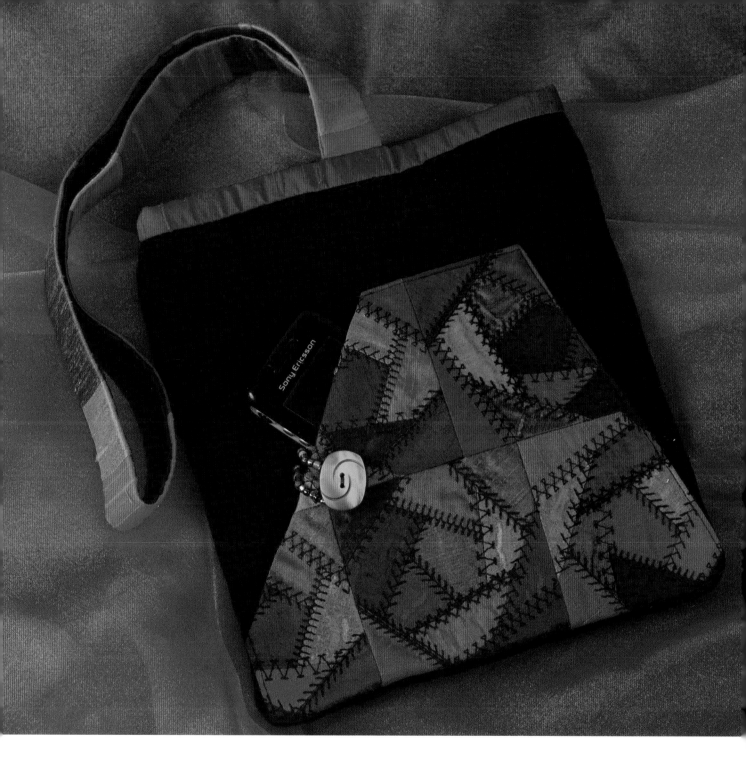

CHAPTER 1

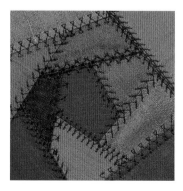

The Essentials

Thanks to technology, piecing using a sewing machine or an embroidery machine has come together to offer the ultimate piecing experience. From simple step-by-step instructions to a CD packed full of printable files, you'll have fun creating blocks for more than a dozen creative projects that line the pages of this book. Complete step-by-step instructions can be found on the enclosed CD.

Foundation Piecing

Thanks to technology, foundation piecing can be accomplished on both a sewing machine and an embroidery machine. An embroidery machine adds an automatic element that can be a timesaver.

The techniques are different for each method, but the results are the same. Foundation piecing makes precision seams. Difficult-to-piece intersections are made easy with this technique. The end results are accurately pieced blocks every time.

Sewing machine piecing starts with a paper foundation, whereas embroidery machine piecing starts with a hooped stabilizer foundation. Each block pattern or design section is numbered to indicate the order in which the fabrics are to be joined to the foundation. On a sewing machine, the seamlines are manually sewn after the fabric is in position. On an embroidery machine the seamlines are automatically embroidered after the fabric is in position. Once the blocks are completed, trim the fabrics and foundation using the outermost perimeter line as a

guide. Once all the blocks are completed, use a sewing machine to sew the blocks together. A sampler of creative projects ideas using pieced blocks are featured on the CD.

All you need to get started is on the CD inside the book back cover. There are individual printable PDF pattern files for sewing machine piecing and individual embroidery designs for embroidery machine piecing. Included are bonus appliqué and quilting designs for use with an embroidery machine.

Copyright

The embroidery designs included in this book are original and protected by the copyright laws. You may use the designs for personal use and for gifts or items

to sell, but sharing, trading or copying them is illegal. Following the copyright protection law will ensure a steady supply of new and creative designs for the

future. For more information about the copyright protection law, log onto www. embroideryprotection.org.

Design Details

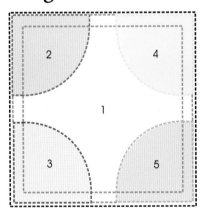
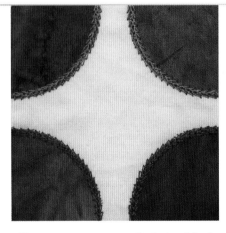

Starting on page 40, the Design Details section offers information about the printable piecing patterns and embroidery designs. The first column indicates the block shape, the number of fabrics required and the fabric placement by number. The second column shows what the individual design will look like when pieced and the third column shows what a four-patch of the designs would look like sewn together. Additional information includes the block size including seam allowances, the starting piece size of the fabric for section 1 and how wide to cut the fabric strips.

There are two types of piecing blocks on the CD: 1) a single pattern or design requiring only one round of fabric piecing to complete the block and 2) a single pattern or design requiring multiple rounds of fabric piecings or hoopings to complete the block. The finished block size is different for both. The complete block size for a single pattern or hooping is 3½" square. The complete block size for a multiple pattern or hooping is 6½" square.

PDF PATTERN FILES

To access the sewing machine piecing patterns, insert the CD into the computer. Use the Design Details to determine the pattern file name. Access the CD using the computer operating system. Copy and save the folder with the pattern PDF files to the computer and print from this file. Print as many copies as required to complete a project onto foundation paper. For more information on Sewing Machine Piecing, refer to Chapter 2, starting on page 13.

EMBROIDERY DESIGNS

A computer and embroidery machine-compatible software are necessary to use the embroidery machine designs. Refer to the owner's manual or consult your local machine dealer honoring your warranty to determine how to retrieve the designs and load them onto your embroidery machine.

The designs are in folders according to the machine brand file format. Using a computer, save the design files directly to the hard drive. Then, use a cable, disk, jump drive or memory card to transfer the designs to your embroidery machine following the manufacturer's instructions.

Most of the designs are for a standard-sized 4" square hoop. However, there are a few that are oversized and require a 5" x 7" hoop or larger. It is best to stitch designs in size-appropriate hoops. Refer to the Design Details, starting on page 43, for design size information. Use these details to choose a hoop size available with your equipment.

Enlarging or reducing the design sizes can be accomplished on the touch-screen of the embroidery machine or using embroidery software. The pieced block size for a standard-sized 4" square hoop is 3½". When sewn to coordinating blocks, the finished block size is 3". Seam allowances have been built into the embroidery designs. Enlarging or reducing the design size will alter the seam allowances. It is best to use editing software to reposition or enlarge the perimeter line to accommodate the size change. The outermost perimeter line is ¼" away from the seamline. It indicates the piece or block cutting line. The innermost perimeter line is .10" larger than the seamline perimeter, so it will not show when blocks are sewn together.

MIRROR-IMAGING

Original triangle border (left) mirror-imaged horizontally.

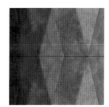

Triangle border mirror-imaged and rotated 180 degrees.

The sewing machine piecing patterns are already mirror-imaged, as the seam stitching is completed on one side of the paper and the fabric layers are placed on another. Some embroidery machine piecing designs will require mirror-imaging in software or on the touch-screen of the embroidery machine. Be sure to be aware of designs that require mirror-imaging when stitching multiple files.

Some designs can be mirror-imaged and rotated 180 degrees to be sewn together creatively. Experiment with design rotation on the computer in embroidery software or the touch-screen of an embroidery machine.

Sewing machine piecing makes rotating a little easier by simply stitching on the right or wrong side of the paper and changing the fabric order. Transparent vellum paper and its see-through properties can make pattern rotation simple.

Test-Stitching

The testing of a new technique should never be missed. It helps to determine if the correct fabric, needle, thread and supplies have been chosen to properly complete the techniques. You will always be test-stitching the design before adding fabric!

For sewing machine piecing, test the foundation, needle, thread and pattern to determine if the appropriate stitch length has been chosen.

For embroidery machine piecing, the first step is to pre-embroider the stitching lines with white thread on the foundation stabilizer.

General Supplies

The supplies are similar for both sewing machine and embroidery machine piecing. However, there is enough difference between the two that the information to follow has been separated by each method.

SEWING MACHINE PIECING

The following supplies will help ensure success when piecing with your sewing machine.

Foundation

Sewing machine piecing starts with a good foundation, as it keeps stitches from stretching when sewn. From paper to fabric, there are a variety of foundations for this technique.

For the piecing patterns and techniques in this book, use paper as the foundation printed from the PDF files on the CD.

Transparent vellum paper found at an office supply store is the most versatile and offers a see-through property, allowing the fabric layers to be visible on both sides. It holds up well to sewing machine stitching and makes the paper piecing process easier. The seam allowances must be trimmed no less than a ¼", ensuring the pieced segment seams will hold together long after the project is constructed.

For those who prefer fabric foundations, use the pattern files on the CD to print directly onto inkjet paper found at your local sewing machine or fabric retailer.

Thread

Use the same weight thread in the needle and the bobbin. For best results, use a cotton or polyester 50- to 80-weight thread. If a pre-wound bobbin is used, match the thread weight to the bobbin for smooth stitching.

For crazy quilting hand-stitches, use traditional pearl cotton. Consult your favorite crazy quilting book for more information on crazy quilting by hand techniques and stitches.

Ignore the thread colors for each stop. Use white or cream thread color for all seamlines. The color stops are the same

for each design. Seam 1 is the same for all design files. This will help identify where you're at in the stitching process for each design, no matter the block name.

Needles

Use a 90/14 embroidery needle with a machine stitch length of 1.5mm to 2mm or 15 to 18 stitches per inch. The needle will help to perforate the paper, making it easier to remove. Test-stitch seams onto vellum and fabric to determine the longest stitch length that can be used to adequately perforate the paper.

Scissors

Use snips to trim threads near the beginning and end of seams. Use a paper scissors to trim the vellum ¼" away from the outermost perimeter line. After piecing, use a rotary cutter, mat and ruler to trim the layers on the outermost perimeter line on the pattern printed side.

Quick Hints for Using Foundation

- Use pins to secure the fabric layers.

- Keep the paper in place until after the project is finished.

- The outermost seam allowance paper may be removed for ease in sewing the blocks together.

- Use a tweezers to carefully remove the paper from interior sections and between stitches.

EMBROIDERY MACHINE PIECING

Unlike sewing machine piecing, embroidery machine piecing requires products that can withstand the stitching speed and automatic features of a digitized design. For best results, use products manufactured for the embroidery machine process.

Stabilizers

There are a multitude of stabilizers appropriate for the foundation of embroidery machine piecing. The foundation needs to hold up to hooping and the machine stitching speeds.

A tear-away, cut-away or water-soluble stabilizer can be used as the foundation for this technique.

Sewing machine foundation papers cannot be easily hooped, as they tend to tear and are not advisable to use for embroidery machine piecing.

Jeanine recommends: Use pre-cut stabilizers slightly larger than the hoop size. Make a stack. Use the last piece in the stack as a template when it comes time to cut more. Be sure to use paper scissors to cut stabilizers, as they will dull fabric scissors.

For a removable foundation, use a clean-tearing stabilizer. Do not tear it away until the blocks have been sewn together. The tear-away stabilizer keeps the blocks in shape during construction. The seam allowances must be trimmed no less than a ¼", ensuring the seams will hold up long after the project is completed. A tear-away stabilizer is not as stiff as paper and may add some strain on the stitches during removal. Remove the stabilizer with care and use a tweezers, if necessary, to remove small pieces from a project.

Another option for a removable foundation is a cut-away water-soluble stabilizer. The stabilizer will remain with the design, but when the project is washed, this type of stabilizer washes away. The seam allowances must be trimmed no less than a ¼", ensuring the seams will hold up long after the project is completed. The use of a cut-away water-soluble is great for vintage piecing where the foundation or batting is flannel or cotton. The layers shrink to create a vintage appearance.

The most versatile foundation is a lightweight cut-away stabilizer. By using a very lightweight, smooth surface cut-away, the stabilizer remains with the blocks and adds stability. It also eliminates the need to tear away the stabilizer when the project is complete. A cut-away also helps to hold the fabric layers secure, as the fabric tends to grip the stabilizer, allowing for easy piecing. When piecing with a thin layer of batting, the cut-away keeps all the layers together. The seam allowances can be trimmed close to the stitching within a ⅛" as the foundation remains to hold the seams secure.

Threads

It is important to use threads of even weight in both the needle and the bobbin. Machine embroidery piecing requires a lot of thread.

Even though the seam embroidery is straight stitched lines, the hoop is removed from the machine after each line is embroidered. The needle thread can be clipped as usual, but depending on the size hoop, the bobbin thread can't be cut until the hoop is off the machine. The larger the hoop, the more bobbin thread is pulled away from the machine. Pre-wound bobbins, if available for your machine, are the most economical and time saving product to use for this technique.

Match the needle thread type to the bobbin. For nylon-type bobbin thread, use a 40- to 50-weight rayon thread. For cotton-type bobbin thread, use a 50- to 60-weight cotton thread. Sewing machine thread can be used, but test for compatibility before starting the piecing process.

The crazy patch piecing technique has specifically digitized decorative stitches similar to crazy quilting stitches done by hand. For best results in duplicating the stitches on the embroidery machine, use 30-weight cotton in a 90/14 size needle. If a larger weight thread is preferred, use a larger needle and slow the machine speed to adequately embroider the stitches.

Jeanine recommends: Cotton variegated threads are great for quilting and decorative crazy quilt stitching. Some variegated threads have a watercolor stitching effect with a seamlessness where one color stops and another color begins. Some variegated threads have a striping effect. Test-stitch variegated threads to see what blend of colors look best for just the right finishing touch.

Needles

For standard piecing, use a 75/11 embroidery needle.

When using a heavier-weight thread, use a larger needle. A heavier thread requires a larger needle and a slower machine speed to properly embroider the decorative stitches. It may be necessary to increase the bobbin thread weight as well.

Use a 90/14 needle when using 30-weight cotton thread for crazy patch quilting.

For 12-cotton thread, use a topstitching needle of size 100/16 or larger.

Test-stitch the decorative designs before starting a project.

Scissors

There are a variety of scissors needed for this technique.

Use a double-curved (tip and handle) embroidery scissors to snip threads on and off the machine. The scissors' curves help clear the hoop and allow for trimming close to the fabric.

Use a fine fabric scissors to cut fabric into strips the size required for the numbered segment.

Use a paper scissors or a rotary cutter, mat and ruler to cut stabilizers. Stabilizers can have a tendency to dull fabric scissors. Save your fabric scissors for cutting fabric and use a paper scissors to cut stabilizers.

Mark scissors to distinguish the difference or purchase paper scissors with colored handles for easy identification.

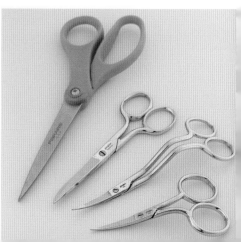

Adhesives

The use of adhesives can be helpful with embroidery machine piecing. The fabric for segment 1 can be sprayed on the wrong side with temporary adhesive. Another option is to use a fabric glue stick to hold it in place. The fabric, when using a cut-away stabilizer, tends to adhere well without any extra help. Use your finger gently to make sure the fabric is secure while the perimeter stitches of segment 1 are embroidered.

For appliqué, fusible web or double-sided adhesive web are alternatives to temporary spray adhesives. Use templates printed from embroidery software to determine the exact size of the appliqué. Cut the web slightly smaller and iron it to the appliqué back. Use a craft iron to secure the appliqué to the hooped fabric within the embroidered outline.

> ***Jeanine recommends:*** *A stiletto can be used to hold fabrics secure when not using an adhesive to hold layers together for embroidery machine piecing. The fiber connection between a permanent, cut-away stabilizer and prewashed fabric can sometimes be enough to hold layers together without shifting. If shifting starts to occur during embroidery, a stiletto can be used to smooth the path for the needle to stitch.*

Pressing Matters

For both sewing and embroidery machine piecing, pressing of the seams is an important part of the process. After sewing or embroidery of each individual segment seam, press the seam open or to the appropriate segment number on the fabric right side.

Although an ironing board and large iron are great for pressing large items, the pieces that are sewn or embroidered in this book are small. Use a small craft iron and pressing board for the individual segment seams and a large iron and pressing board for completed blocks and projects.

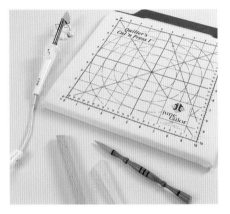

IRONING SURFACES

Set up a pressing station next to your sewing or embroidery machine. A small table at a 90-degree angle from the table your sewing or embroidery machine sits on is ideal. Sew or embroider the seam and turn to your right or left to press the seam.

There are some ironing stations that hook directly to a table. The only requirement will be an extra outlet for the craft iron. Sewing and embroidery machines should be hooked up to a serge protector, which would have additional outlets for a light and iron. Take advantage of the extra outlets for machines, lighting and pressing to make the piecing process simple.

OTHER PRESSING OPTIONS

There are a variety of items that can be used instead of a mini-iron to press seams. Try a specially made pressing wooden stick with a sharp flat edge to smooth seams flat. Be sure not to tug or pull on the fabric. Use a hard, flat surface with the wooden sticks to press allowances flat. A seam roller is another option for pressing seams flat. Both require a heavy hand and a bit of muscle. Piecing can be considered a muscle-builder, too!

Fabrics

The selection of fabrics suitable for piecing is astounding. A variety of fibers will work well for this technique. The most common fabric is quilt-making cotton. The colors. in prints to batiks to solids, can transform piecework into artwork.

For best results, pre-wash and dry cotton fabrics to remove sizing and raise fibers. Clean finish the raw edges of small pieces with a serger to prevent unraveling during the laundry process. The raised fibers tend to "grab" and hold fabrics and foundation layers together. Hand-dyed fabrics can be used without pretreatment, along with many batik fabrics. These fabrics have already gone through a water-wash and are ready to piece.

CHOOSING COLORS

Fabric colors make a difference in the finished block's overall appearance. Small fabric pieces are used for foundation piecing. Use leftover pieces from a quilt-making project or purchase new coordinating pieces.

Quilt fabric stores sometimes offer fabric fat-quarter or fat-eighth bundles in a collection of coordinating fabrics. These bundles make piecing easy. Cut strips from each fabric piece in the bundle and lay the fabrics out in the order in which the fabrics were bundled. If there are only seven colors in the bundle and there are nine sections in the pattern, start over with the first and second pieces for sections 8 and 9. The next block can start with the third fabric in the bundle, making no two blocks the same.

Most quilt fabric manufacturers produce fabric lines consisting of multiple

Crazy Patch 2 with solid fabric and decorative embroidery stitches.

Crazy Patch 2 with black-and-white print fabric, no decorative stitching and an attractive embroidery design in the center.

coordinating fabrics. The fabric bolt end contains the manufacturer name, fabric line name and color. Search a quilt fabric shop for coordinating pieces or ask the shop owner for help in finding the fabric line. Some shops have collections sorted together on the shelf, which makes fabric selection a breeze.

To cut down on piecing labor, add solid fabric blocks and sashing between and around pieced blocks. Be sure to purchase extra fabric for sashing, borders, backing and binding to finish constructing the project.

GRAIN

The fabric grain isn't as important with foundation piecing as it is with other quilt piecing methods. The small fabric sections are sewn onto a foundation that will keep the fabrics in shape during the piecing process. Keeping the foundation in place during project construction also keeps the fabrics in shape. Not until the project is complete should the foundation be removed, if using a temporary foundation.

The great part about using a cut-away foundation with embroidery machine piecing is the foundation is permanent and will remain with the project, keeping the fabrics in alignment.

The fabric grain only matters when using plaids, checks and stripes. For best results, use fabrics with vertical patterns in their design.

MEASURING AND CUTTING

Use the Design Details, starting on page 43, as a guide for cutting fabric strips. A rotary cutter, mat and ruler can make this process easy. Fat quarters are 18" along the selvedge by anywhere from 20" to 22½" wide (depending on the fabric width). Fold the fat quarter in half along the selvedge edge to make 9" x 22½" pieces. Cut off the selvedge to prevent accidental use. Determine the strip sizes

and cut strips along the selvedge edge. Cut strips in sections to increase piecing speed.

Each fabric piece needs to be large enough to cover the pattern or design numbered area plus the seam allowances. Be generous. The Design Details has the general sizes to cut strips, but if you want to cut strips for each numbered

section, use a tape measure or small ruler to measure each section. Print the PDF files of the patterns (note the patterns are mirror-imaged), print templates from embroidery software, or stitch the entire design outline onto stabilizer to measure for fabric strips or pieces. Cut strips or pieces ¾" to 1" wider than the widest point of the section. For speed, cut strips for the two largest sections.

Cutting Triangles

Triangles require more fabric when piecing into a block. Either measure the triangle at its widest width and cut strips that wide, or use one of the following two options.

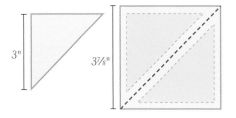
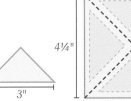

Option 1 (use for half-square triangles):

1. Measure the short side of the triangle.

2. Cut a square ⅞" larger than the measurement from step 1.

3. Cut the square in half diagonally to create two triangles the size needed for piecing.

Option 2 (use for quarter-square triangles):

1. Measure the long side of the triangle.

2. Cut a square 1¼" larger than the measurement from step 1.

3. Cut the square in quarters diagonally to create four triangles the size needed for piecing.

BATTING, BACKING AND BINDING

Batting can be added before or after piecing.

For a raised effect to embroidery machine-pieced fabrics, use a very thin layer of polyester batting on top of the stabilizer and piece fabrics directly to the batting and stabilizer layers.

Use a low-loft batting whenever possible. For the vintage look, use a cotton batting.

Back your projects with batting and backing. Use the bonus Quilting Designs on the CD to hold the layers together or use a straight stitch and a clear monofilament thread to stitch in the ditch of the block seams.

Bind projects using your preferred method. Refer to your favorite quilt instruction book for more information and detailed instructions.

The CD contains 12 great projects for piecing, like those shown above. Use the projects to jumpstart your piecing fun!

CHAPTER 2

Sewing Machine Piecing

Whether piecing by sewing machine or embroidery machine, the results are the same—fantastic projects. Complete step-by-step instructions can be found on the CD included on the inside back cover of this book.

Sewing Machine Piecing Basics

Traditional sewing machine paper-piecing is the foundation for embroidery machine piecing. For those without an embroidery machine, the blocks and projects featured in this book can be created using the printable patterns found on the CD and a sewing machine.

It is necessary to have Adobe Acrobat Reader software to access the files. This software usually comes preloaded with the purchase of a computer. If not, the software is free and downloadable at www.adobe.com.

Each pattern section is numbered to indicate the order in which the fabrics are to be sewn to the foundation. The stitching lines are in color, making them identifiable and easy to follow for each segment.

Use the Design Details, starting on page 43, to reference the pattern file name, block size, starting piece size (section 1) and the width to cut strips. To access the printable patterns, insert the CD inside the back cover into the computer. The disk is read-only, so use your operating system to access the CD and open the folder labeled Sewing Machine Piecing. Print the patterns directly from the disk, or copy the files to a folder on your computer and then print the patterns.

The foundation used for sewing machine piecing is different than embroidery machine piecing. Sewing machine piecing is stitched on paper, while embroidery machine piecing uses a stabilizer.

There are many different types of paper that can be used. From water-soluble to copy machine or printer paper, translucent vellum paper is the most versatile. It holds up well to stitching and folding, and is readily available from office supply stores. Be sure the packaging indicates the printer type for use.

Determine how many blocks are required for the project and print that many paper pattern sheets. The non-printed side is for fabric placement, and the printed side is for stitching.

The patterns can be reduced or enlarged using a copy machine. PDF files cannot be edited without appropriate software. Therefore, to make size changes, print the patterns onto plain paper (do not use the vellum) and use a color copy machine to reduce or enlarge the pattern as desired. Or, depending on your photo or graphic software capabilities, print and then scan the pattern into software to make size changes. Note that the seam allowances are set for the pattern size in this book. When enlarging or reducing patterns, it is important to draw boundary lines. The gray line is 1/16" away from the actual seamline (so it doesn't show in the seam). Measure 1/4" from the gray line and draw a new black line representing the block trimming line.

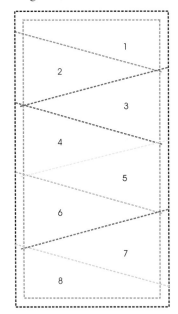

The patterns on the CD are mirror-imaged (reversed) for sewing machine piecing, as the seam stitching is completed on the pattern-printed side and the fabric is placed on the other side to form an accurately pieced block. When creating your own paper-piecing patterns in software, be sure the images are mirror-imaged before printing.

Use the same thread and weight in the bobbin as in the needle (between 50- and 80-weight). For best results, use a 90/14 embroidery needle. The larger needle will help perforate the vellum and allow for easier removal once the project is finished. Removal of the paper from the outermost seam allowance is helpful in sewing blocks together; do not remove the paper from the entire block until the project is complete. This helps to keep the blocks stable and in shape for assembly.

Set the sewing machine stitch length to 15 to 18 stitches per inch or 1.5 to 2mm. The larger machine needle will help to stitch larger holes in the paper to aid in tearing vellum cleanly from the seams.

It is important to reverse-stitch to lock the seams when beginning and ending. The pressure of tearing away the paper foundation can cause stress on the seams. The reinforcement of the stitches keeps the seams stable.

If necessary, use pins to hold the fabric layers in place before stitching. Remove the pins before coming in contact with the needle.

Keep pressing to a minimum with a small craft iron, as the ink on the paper could smear. An option is to use a pressing roller or a wooden pressing stick on a firm surface. Do not touch the iron to the paper.

The smooth surface of the vellum paper makes the layers slippery. Fabrics tend to move or shift when handled, requiring the use of pins or a fabric glue stick.

Use a rotary cutter, mat and ruler to trim the excess fabric after stitching to a 1/4" seam allowance. Avoid trimming closer than the 1/4". The seam structure in sewing machine piecing must support itself as the foundation is removed after the blocks are sewn together.

Step-by-Step Instructions

Try this technique with the Triangle Border pattern.

Note: The piecing process involves steps 1 through 10, and then as each fabric layer is added, steps 7, 9 and 10 are repeated throughout.

1. Print the Triangle Border pattern onto vellum paper.

2. Cut fabric strips the size indicated in the Design Details on page 46 (2" x 4½").

3. Use a rotary cutter, ruler and mat to trim the pattern ¼" from the outermost dashed line (black).

4. Layer two cut strips, right sides together (fabric for sections 1 and 2).

5. Lay the pattern with the paper-printed side up on the fabric ¼" over the line between sections 1 and 2. The vellum is opaque and allows for transparent placement.

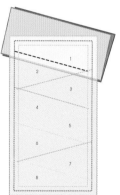

6. Hold or pin the layers together and sew directly on the stitching line (green). Pins help hold fabrics in place when flipping the pattern over to sew the seams.

7. Press the fabric open on the fabric side of the pattern toward the respective numbers; do not touch the pattern paper with the iron.

8. Turn the pattern over to the printed side and fold the pattern on the line between sections 2 and 3 (blue).

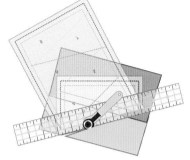

9. Use a rotary cutter, ruler and mat to trim the excess fabric, leaving a ¼" seam allowance.

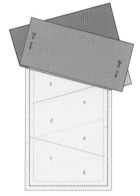

10. Position the next fabric layer on the fabric side of the pattern, right sides together, matching raw edges and pin to hold the layers together.

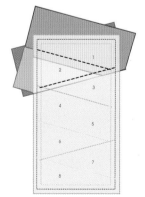

11. Turn the pattern over to the printed side and stitch on the line between sections 2 and 3 (blue).

12. Repeat step 7 (press fabric open).

13. Turn the pattern over to the printed side and fold the pattern on the line between sections 3 and 4 (red).

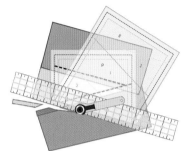

14. Repeat step 9 (trim excess fabric).

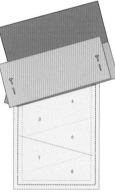

15. Repeat step 10 (position next fabric piece).

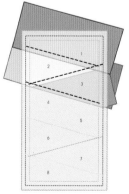

16. Turn the pattern over to the printed side and stitch on the line between sections 3 and 4 (red).

15

17. Repeat step 7 (press fabric open).

18. Turn the pattern over to the printed side and fold the pattern on the line between sections 4 and 5 (yellow).

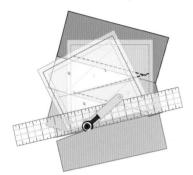

19. Repeat step 9 (trim excess fabric).

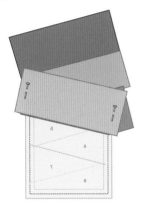

20. Repeat step 10 (position next fabric piece).

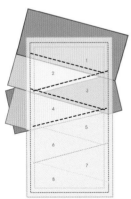

21. Turn the pattern over to the printed side and stitch on the line between sections 4 and 5 (yellow).

22. Repeat step 7 (press fabric open).

23. Turn the pattern over to the printed side and fold the pattern on the line between sections 5 and 6 (mint green).

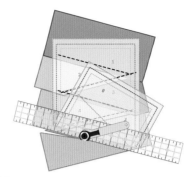

24. Repeat step 9 (trim excess fabric).

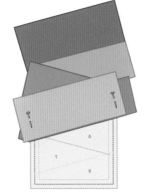

25. Repeat step 10 (position next fabric piece).

26. Turn the pattern over to the printed side and stitch on the line between sections 5 and 6 (mint green).

27. Repeat step 7 (press fabric open).

28. Turn the pattern over to the printed side and fold the pattern on the line between sections 6 and 7 (purple).

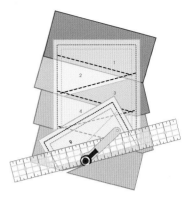

29. Repeat step 9 (trim excess fabric).

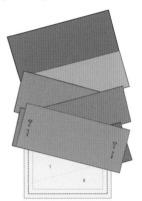

30. Repeat step 10 (position next fabric piece).

31. Turn the pattern over to the printed side and stitch on the line between sections 6 and 7 (purple).

32. Repeat step 7 (press fabric open).

33. Turn the pattern over to the printed side and fold the pattern on the line between sections 7 and 8 (lime green).

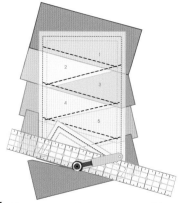

34. Repeat step 9 (trim excess fabric).

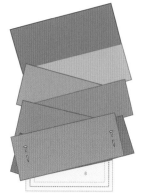

35. Repeat step 10 (position next fabric piece).

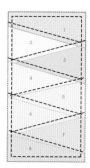

36. Turn the pattern over to the printed side and stitch on the line between sections 7 and 8 (lime green).

37. Repeat step 7 (press fabric open).

38. Stitch directly on the inner border (gray), holding the layers together.

39. Trim the block on the outer border (black).

40. Repeat these steps for additional Triangle Border blocks.

Sewing Machine Challenges

There will be some designs more difficult to complete on the sewing machine, such as the Doll and Coffee Cup. Both have additional embroidery machine stitch details. To obtain the same look as the embroidery machine stitching, embellish the blocks with hand or sewing machine stitching. The Doll arms can be satin stitches tapered from 4mm to 1mm. The Coffee Cup steam stitching can be created using a straight stretch stitch.

The raw-edge appliqué stitches for the "Applipiecing" blocks (Corner Circles, Crooked Squares, Purse and Wheel) can be completed with traditional satin stitches or any one of the decorative stitches on your sewing machine. Slow the machine speed and stitch carefully over the raw edges with a 3mm or wider stitch width. Use a tear-away stabilizer for a smaller-width decorative stitch like the embroidery machine version shown.

The Crazy Patch blocks will be the most fun because decorative hand or machine stitches can be used. Many sewing machines have stitches that resemble hand embroidery. Experiment with stitches on extra fabric to view the stitch detail closely. Once satisfied with the stitches, sew directly over the seamline on the pieced block.

For best results on decorative stitches, use a 30-weight embroidery cotton or rayon thread in the needle. Keep a lighter weight thread in the bobbin. A slight tension adjustment might be necessary. If a heavier hand-embroidered look is desired, use a 16/100 needle or higher with a 12-weight cotton or wool thread. The thicker the thread, the more it appears hand-stitched. Consult your favorite crazy quilting stitch book for hand-stitching techniques.

Sewing Blocks Together

Use pins to hold individual blocks together while sewing seams. Align blocks together, matching pieced sections. Pin at points where matching matters. Where seams meet, pin directly into both seams to ensure precise alignment.

Press seams open when sewing blocks together. This will keep layers as flat as possible for quilting layers together.

Remove pins before coming in contact with the needle. Do not sew over pins, as it can alter the machine timing and potentially break pins, which could cause bodily harm.

CHAPTER 3
Embroidery Machine Piecing

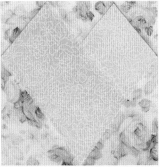

Use the traditional block designs to create bands around buckets, holders, boxes or planters. Simply seam one-hooping blocks together, back with a fabric piece cut to size, seam the wrap and bind the raw edges. Complete step-by-step instructions can be found on the CD included on the inside back cover of this book.

Embroidery Machine Piecing Basics

Embroidery machine piecing was born from the desire to automate sewing machine foundation piecing.

When working with small fabric pieces and sharp corners, nothing is more precise than foundation piecing and it can be accomplished much faster with an embroidery machine.

The Crooked Log Cabin design requires only one hooping to complete the block.

There are four types of embroidery machine piecing designs on the enclosed CD. Traditional quilt blocks are the most common to foundation piecing. Carrying on this tradition, there are 11 designs in this grouping. Seven designs are complete blocks pieced in one hooping on the embroidery machine and four designs require four hoopings to make a complete block.

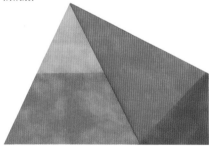

The Windmill design requires four hoopings to complete the block.

Each block section is numbered to indicate the order in which the fabrics are to be embroidered. Use the Design Details, starting on page 40, to reference the design file name, block size, starting piece size (section 1) and the width to cut strips.

To access the designs, insert the CD from the inside the back cover into the computer. The disk is read-only, so use your operating system to access the CD and open the folder labeled Embroidery Machine Piecing. Copy the design files to a folder on your computer and then transfer the designs to your embroidery machine according to your owner's manual.

The foundation used for embroidery machine piecing is different than sewing machine piecing. Embroidery machine piecing requires the use of stabilizer.

The technique will determine if a temporary or permanent stabilizer is used for the blocks. Consider the following:

- If the stabilizer will be a permanent foundation, use a cut-away and trim the seam allowances close to the stitching line.

- If the stabilizer will be a temporary foundation, use a tear-away and trim the seam allowances to a ¼".

- If a separate fabric piece will be the foundation, use a tear-away stabilizer.

Additional layering methods are explored in Chapter 6: Creative Piecing, starting on page 34.

A temporary stabilizer must tear cleanly without harming the stitches. The stabilizer should not be removed until the entire project is finished. Stabilizer helps keep the blocks stable and in shape for assembly. Multiple stitching lines in the same area will prematurely break down a tear-away stabilizer, which could pose a problem with alignment. Be sure to test-stitch to find the right stabilizer.

Using a very lightweight permanent stabilizer is preferred for embroidery machine piecing, as it stays with the fabric, allows for decorative stitching without additional support, and seam allowances can be kept to a minimum, preventing dark fabric from showing through light fabric.

Use embroidery thread of similar or equal weights in the needle and bobbin. A smooth, lightweight thread will keep the embroidery stitches from building up through the layers. For best results, use a natural fiber thread, such as cotton or rayon, in basic colors.

> *Jeanine suggests:* Forward through the design manually using the machine touch-screen. Move the needle to the first stitch past the jump. This will aid in determining where the seam starts and save on thread use.

Embroidery machine piecing uses a lot of bobbin thread when taking the hoop on and off the machine between seamline stitching. Either stock up on pre-wound bobbins (check with your machine dealer for compatibility), or pre-wind multiple bobbins.

A 75/11 needle should be used for piecing, but switch to a 90/14 needle for decorative stitching with a 30-weight thread or a 100/16 needle with 12-weight thread.

Use a double-curved embroidery scissors to trim the fabric in the hoop. Trim closely when using cut-away stabilizer or fabric as the foundation. Trim all but ¼" away from the seamline when using a tear-away stabilizer as the foundation.

Having a craft iron and pressing surface close to the embroidery machine will make the block easier to stitch. In most cases after embroidering a segment, the hoop will be removed from the machine and placed on an ironing surface to press the fabric toward the foundation. Depending on the foundation, sometimes the pressing can be eliminated and a fabric glue stick can be used to hold the layers in place. For best results, use a craft iron to smooth the seamlines and fabric in place.

The designs can be reduced or enlarged depending on your machine and software capabilities. Some machines and software have the capabilities of resizing a design while altering the stitch count. Others simply make the stitches smaller or larger. It is best to enlarge or reduce designs when the stitch count is altered to compensate for the size. It may be necessary to adjust the outer perimeter lines, which are the block trimming and fabric basting lines. The outermost line is the block size before assembly. It needs to be ¼" from the seamline. For best results, enlarge or reduce designs in software where the individual lines can moved and altered to compensate for size changes.

Step-by-Step Instructions

Try this technique with the Star design.

Note: Instructions are for using a cut-away stabilizer as the foundation. Also, the piecing process involves steps 1 through 11, and then as each fabric layer is added, steps 7, 10 and 11 are repeated throughout.

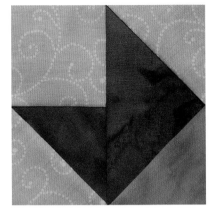

1. Load the Star design onto the touch-screen of your embroidery machine.

2. Hoop the stabilizer.

Jeanine says:
When using a cut-away stabilizer, it is OK to trim closely—up to ⅛" away from the stitching line. The seam is sewn to a permanent foundation and will not be subject to pulling or stress.

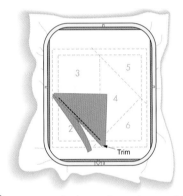

3. Stitch the entire design without fabric. Turn off the machine "stops," if your machine has this feature, but don't forget to turn the "stops" back on after this step. Watch the design stitch to identify the steps for fabric placement.

4. Remove the hoop from the machine. Cut a piece of fabric large enough to cover section 1. Be generous with your fabric cutting.

5. Place the fabric over the area. Return the hoop to the machine and stitch segment 2.

Jeanine suggests: Trim darker-colored fabrics close to the stitching when under a lighter fabric. To prevent show-through, trim lighter-colored fabrics over darker fabrics wider.

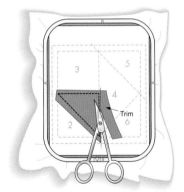

6. Remove the hoop from the machine, but do not unhoop the fabric. Trim the excess fabric away from the stitching lines on all sides.

7. Cut a piece of fabric large enough to cover section 2 plus the seam allowances. Be sure the fabric extends beyond the stitching perimeter lines.

8. Place the fabric over the stitching line between sections 1 and 2.

9. Return the hoop to the machine and stitch segment 3.

10. Remove the hoop from the machine and trim close to the stitching.

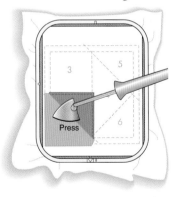

11. Place on an ironing surface and press the fabric open toward section 2.

12. Repeat step 7 (cut a piece of fabric large enough to cover section 3).

13. Place the fabric over the stitching line between sections 1 and 3.

14. Return the hoop to the machine and stitch segment 4.

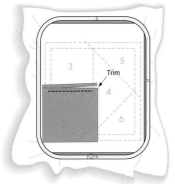

15. Repeat step 10 (trim close to the stitching).

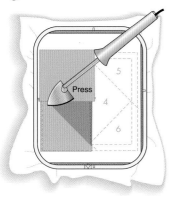

16. Repeat step 11 (press fabric open).

17. Repeat step 7 (cut a piece of fabric large enough to cover section 4).

18. Place the fabric over the stitching line between sections 4 and 3, 1 and 2.

19. Return the hoop to the machine and stitch segment 5.

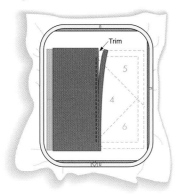

20. Repeat step 10 (trim close to the stitching).

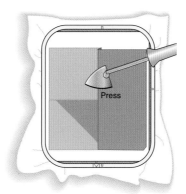

21. Repeat step 11 (press fabric open).

22. Repeat step 7 (cut a piece of fabric large enough to cover section 5).

23. Place the fabric over the stitching line between sections 4 and 5.

24. Return the hoop to the machine and stitch segment 6.

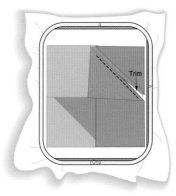

25. Repeat step 10 (trim close to the stitching).

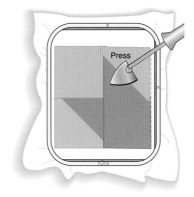

26. Repeat step 11 (press fabric open).

27. Repeat step 7 (cut a piece of fabric large enough to cover section 6).

28. Place the fabric over the stitching line between sections 5 and 6.

29. Return the hoop to the machine and stitch segment 7.

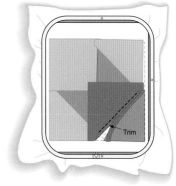

30. Repeat step 10 (trim close to the stitching).

31. Repeat step 11 (press fabric open).

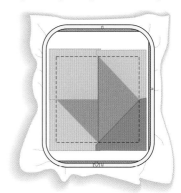

32. Stitch segment 8 (perimeter stitching near seam allowance) while using your fingers to hold the fabrics in place as the machine stitches over the layers.

33. Remove the fabric from the hoop.

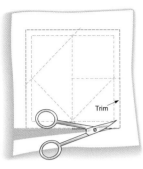

Trim

34. Turn to the stabilizer side of the quarter block and trim directly on the outermost stitching line (3½" square perimeter).

35. Repeat steps 1 through 34 three more times to complete the Star block, as shown above.

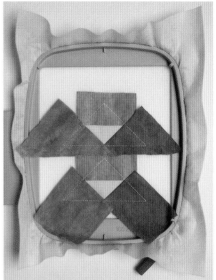

Designs that can be used for this technique:

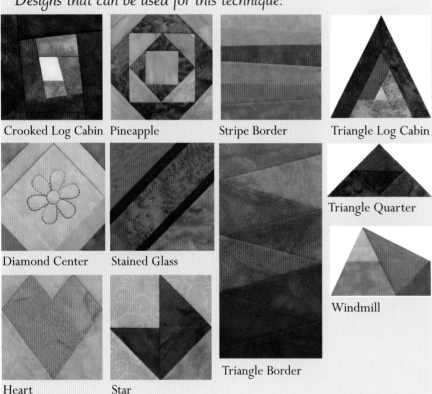

Crooked Log Cabin   Pineapple   Stripe Border   Triangle Log Cabin

Diamond Center   Stained Glass   Triangle Quarter

Windmill

Heart   Star   Triangle Border

Hooping Helpers

Whenever possible, use the smallest size hoop for piecing individual blocks. However, there are some manufacturer hoop sizes that are just large enough to embroider more than one block in a hoop. It is never advisable to use a large hoop for a single small design, but it is possible to use a small hoop to piece two small designs.

To speed up the piecing process, purchase an extra standard-sized hoop. This can be especially beneficial with designs that require mirror-imaging of the block. One hoop can be used for the standard block version and the other hoop can be for the mirror-imaging. This way you will know that you've created one of each to complete the finished block correctly.

Fabric Color Variations

The same number of blocks pieced together look completely different by just changing the number of fabrics. Experiment with a variety of fabrics to create blocks. Use quilting software to add color to blocks on the computer before starting the machine piecing process.

Star design pieced with four fabric colors.   Star design pieced with three fabric colors.

Experiment with light and dark fabric variations. Piece the Triangle Quarter design with two fabrics. Use one light fabric and one dark fabric in the same color family.

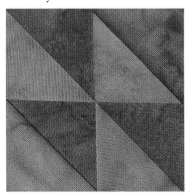

Sew the long ends of a light and dark fabric Triangle Quarter together to create a 2" block. Use the blocks in a small project or use them in conjunction with other pieced blocks.

Sew four light and dark Triangle Quarter sections together—two of each version—to create a 3½" block.

The completed blocks are then sewn together in 90-degree increments to create a light-and-dark variation with only two fabric colors.

Here's the same Triangle Quarter block with four completely different fabric colors pieced together.

Piece and then sew four Triangle Quarter sections together for yet another variation.

Use the Triangle Quarter to piece a border by sewing sections together side-by-side on the diagonal. Continue sewing sections together until the border is long enough for all sides. If the border and sashing are planned correctly, the border will form the perfect miter, connecting the sides together at the corners.

Sew the long ends together to create a 2" block similar to the light-and-dark variation.

Sashing and Borders

To enlarge the block size without enlarging the design, add sashing between individual sections that require four hoopings to complete a block. Add a border in the same fabric color as the sashing.

Star design with sashing between block sections.

Below is the the same block without sashing. The blocks sewn next to each other provide a seamless finished block.

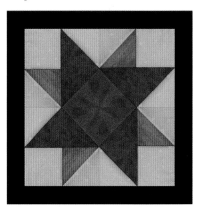

Star design without sashing between block sections.

CHAPTER 4

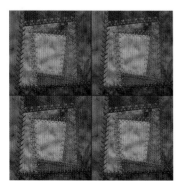

Crazy Patch Piecing

Here's a great project for the favorite man in your life. It's an even more perfect gift if he helped you purchase your embroidery machine! Show off your new creative talents by embroidering and sewing a special gift for him. Include a new wallet in the box along with two tickets to his favorite sports game and enjoy a day away with your favorite guy to say "thank you" for being so wonderful! Complete step-by-step instructions can be found on the CD included on the inside back cover of this book.

Crazy Patch Piecing Basics

Crazy Patch Piecing is perhaps the most versatile piecing group on the CD. There are three designs that are made specifically for crazy patch piecing. Each design requires two files, as the block piecing is created with one design file and the decorative stitching with another. This allows the block piecing design to be used alone or with the decorative stitching—each offering a variety of results.

The decorative stitching can be accomplished with the designs on the CD or by hand. Should you choose to embroider the decorative stitches by hand, consult your favorite crazy quilting book for stitch information.

For embroidery machine piecing, test-stitch the decorative stitches on a pieced sample before starting the project. Use each decorative seam stitching as a chance to test threads. The best thread weights for use on an embroidery machine are a 30-weight or thicker.

Use a heavier needle, such as a 90/14 for a 30-weight or a 100/16 for a 12-

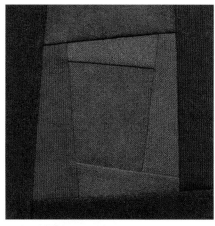

Without decorative stitching, a crazy-pieced block can stand on its own.

With decorative stitching, the variegated thread adds a lot of charm to a block.

weight. The eye of the needle needs to be large enough to accommodate the thread, and the needle needs to be thick enough to penetrate the fabric with the thread to make the stitch complete without breaking either. Slow the machine speed to allow the stitches to form properly.

Variegated threads can create a beautiful array of colors on a crazy patch block. Most thread manufacturers offer variegated threads in a rainbow of color hues. The distance between colors can make a difference in the end results. Color changes that occur far apart in the strand will result in a striped effect. Color changes that occur close together or randomly in color offer a more watercolor effect. Test-stitch variegated threads from an assortment of manufacturers to obtain the look you desire in your stitching.

Step-by-Step Instructions

Try this technique with the Crazy Patch 2 pattern or design. The instructions below detail the steps needed when using your embroidery machine.

For sewing machine piecing, follow the steps found in Chapter 2, pages 15 through 17, substituting the Crazy Patch 2 pattern for the Triangle Border pattern. Use sewing machine decorative stitches to finish the crazy quilting stitches or quilt them by hand.

Note: Instructions are for using a cut-away stabilizer as the foundation. Also, the piecing process involves steps 1 through 11, and then as each fabric layer is added, steps 7, 10 and 11 are repeated throughout.

1. Load the Crazy Patch 2 design onto the touch-screen of your embroidery machine.

2. Hoop the stabilizer.

3. Stitch the entire design without fabric. Turn off the machine "stops," if your machine has this feature, but don't forget to turn the "stops" back on after this step. Watch the design stitch to identify the steps for fabric placement.

4. Remove the hoop from the machine and cut a piece of fabric large enough to cover section 1. Be generous with your fabric cutting.

5. Place the fabric over the area and stitch segment 2.

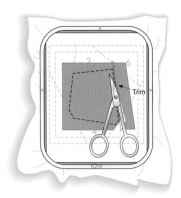

6. Remove the hoop from the machine, but do not unhoop the fabric. Trim the excess fabric away from the stitching lines on all sides.

7. Cut a piece of fabric large enough to cover section 2 plus the seam allowances. Be sure the fabric extends beyond section perimeter stitching lines.

8. Place the fabric over the stitching line between sections 1 and 2.

9. Return the hoop to the machine and stitch segment 3.

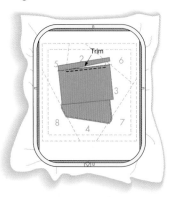

10. Remove the fabric from the hoop and trim close to the stitching.

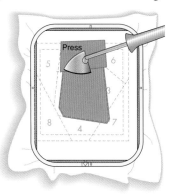

11. Place on an ironing surface and press the fabric open toward section 2.

12. Repeat step 7 (cut a piece of fabric large enough to cover section 3).

13. Place the fabric over the stitching line between sections 1 and 3.

14. Return the hoop to the machine and stitch segment 4.

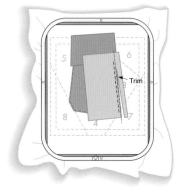

15. Repeat step 10 (trim close to the stitching).

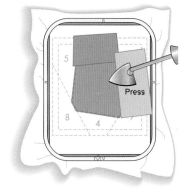

16. Repeat step 11 (press fabric open).

17. Repeat step 7 (cut a piece of fabric large enough to cover section 4).

18. Place the fabric over the stitching line between sections 1 and 4.

19. Return the hoop to the machine and stitch segment 5.

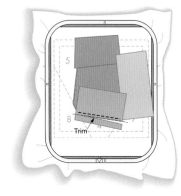

20. Repeat step 10 (trim close to the stitching).

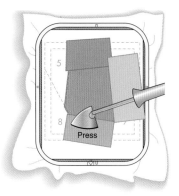

21. Repeat step 11 (press fabric open).

22. Repeat step 7 (cut a piece of fabric large enough to cover section 5).

23. Place the fabric over the stitching line between sections 1, 2 and 5.

24. Return the hoop to the machine and stitch segment 6.

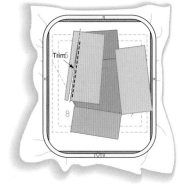

25. Repeat step 10 (trim close to the stitching).

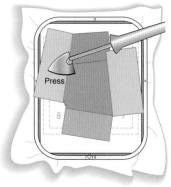

26. Repeat step 11 (press fabric open).

27. Repeat step 7 (cut a piece of fabric large enough to cover section 6).

28. Place the fabric over the stitching line between sections 2, 3 and 6.

29. Return the hoop to the machine and stitch segment 7.

30. Repeat step 10 (trim close to the stitching).

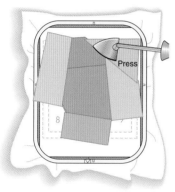

31. Repeat step 11 (press fabric open).

32. Repeat step 7 (cut a piece of fabric large enough to cover section 7).

33. Place the fabric over the stitching line between sections 3, 4 and 7.

34. Return the hoop to the machine and stitch segment 8.

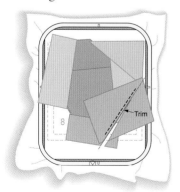

35. Repeat step 10 (trim close to the stitching).

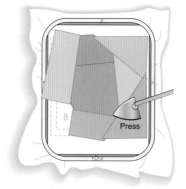

36. Repeat step 11 (press fabric open).

37. Repeat step 7 (cut a piece of fabric large enough to cover section 8).

38. Place the fabric over the stitching line between sections 4, 5 and 8.

39. Return the hoop to the machine and stitch segment 9.

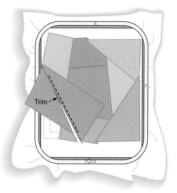

40. Repeat step 10 (trim close to the stitching).

41. Repeat step 11 (press fabric open).

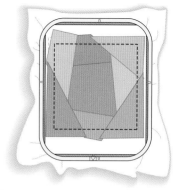

42. Stitch segment 10 (perimeter stitching near seam allowance) while gently using your fingers to keep the fabrics in place as the machine stitches over the layers. Once you have finished this step, the block is complete and ready for the decorative stitching.

43. Keep the hoop on the machine and load the CPQ2 design from the CD.

44. Change the needle to a 14/90, change the thread to a 30-weight and slow the machine speed.

45. Stitch the decorative stitches in all one color or change colors at each color stop. Once you finish this step, your block is complete.

46. Turn the block to the wrong side and trim on the outermost stitching line (3½" square perimeter).

Designs that can be used for this technique:

Crazy Log Cabin

Crazy Patch 1

Crazy Patch 2

Note: Decorative stitches for covering seamlines are found on a separate design file in the Quilting Designs folder on the CD.

CHAPTER 5

Applipiecing

Use a 12" square scrapbooking frame with mat and glass that can be removed to make way for corkboard and your "applipiecing" project. Use colorful sewing machine pins to tack notes up for your family, especially when you've gone shopping for your favorite hobby! Complete step-by-step instructions can be found on the CD included on the inside back cover of this book.

Applipiecing Basics

"Applipiecing" is the combination of appliqué and piecing techniques. The fabric is placed onto the foundation, the stitching line is embroidered, the raw fabric edges are trimmed, another layer is added and decorative machine stitches are embroidered over the raw edges. You are literally piecing and appliquéing fabric onto the foundation. Some of the Applipiecing designs on the CD combine basic embroidery machine piecing with applipiecing to mix up the creativity!

This technique is most successful when using a cut-away stabilizer as the foundation. The stabilizer will remain with the design and keep the stitches secure as all layers are trimmed close to the stitching line. A temporary stabilizer would make the stitched design a bit unstable. The raw edge finishing stitches are not as wide as a standard appliqué stitch, but the end results provide a stable finish to the block when used with a permanent stabilizer.

Use a 30-weight thread and a 90/14 needle to stitch the raw edge finishing stitches. Cotton thread will create a matte finish to the embroidery, whereas a rayon thread will provide a shiny finish; both offer outstanding results.

Use a double-curved embroidery scissors to trim close to the fabric edges. Use one hand to keep the excess fabric upright and use the other to trim close to the stitching.

Step-by-Step Instructions

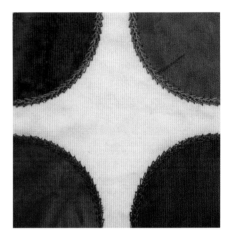

Try this technique with the Corner Circles pattern or design. The instructions below detail the steps needed when using your embroidery machine.

For sewing machine piecing, follow the steps found in Chapter 2, pages 15 through 17, substituting the Corner Circles pattern for the Triangle Border pattern. Use sewing machine decorative stitches to finish the raw edges.

Note: Instructions are for using a cut-away stabilizer as the foundation. Also, the piecing process involves steps 1 through 6, and then as each fabric layer is added, steps 7, 9 and 10 are repeated throughout.

1. Load the Corner Circles design onto the touch-screen of your embroidery machine.

2. Hoop the stabilizer.

3. Stitch the entire design except for the decorative stitching without fabric. Turn off the machine "stops," if your machine has this feature, but don't forget to turn the "stops" back on after this step. Watch the design stitch to identify the steps for fabric placement. Stop the machine before the decorative stitches begin.

4. Remove the hoop from the machine and cut a piece of fabric large enough to cover section 1. Be generous with your fabric cutting.

5. Place the fabric over the area, return the hoop to the machine and stitch segment 2.

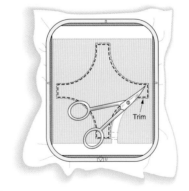

6. Remove the hoop from the machine; do not unhoop the fabric. Trim the excess fabric away, close to the stitching.

7. Cut a piece of fabric large enough to cover section 2 plus the seam allowances. Be sure the fabric extends beyond the section perimeter lines.

8. Place the fabric over section 2.

9. Return the hoop to the machine, change the thread color to match the fabric, or use a clear monofilament thread if desired, and stitch segment 3.

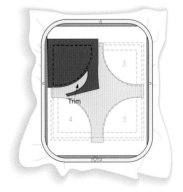

10. Remove the hoop from the machine and trim close to the stitching.

11. Repeat step 7 (cut a piece of fabric large enough to cover section 3).

12. Place the fabric over section 3.

13. Repeat step 9 (stitch segment 4).

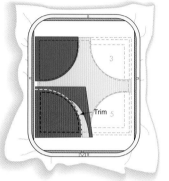

14. Repeat step 10 (trim close to the stitching).

15. Repeat step 7 (cut a piece of fabric large enough to cover section 4).

16. Place the fabric over section 4.

17. Repeat step 9 (stitch segment 5).

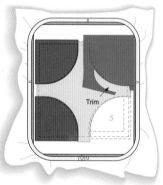

18. Repeat step 10 (trim close to the stitching).

19. Repeat step 7 (cut a piece of fabric large enough to cover section 5).

20. Place the fabric over section 5.

21. Repeat step 9 (stitch segment 6).

The Festive Fabric Basket on the CD is a beautiful holiday project made with the Corner Circles design.

Jeanine recommends: *Various colorful permanent markers come in handy for this technique. When using a natural fiber thread, such as cotton or rayon, in white or ivory colors, the stitching lines can be carefully colored in permanent marker to match the fabric, thus eliminating the need to change thread colors for each fabric. The raw edge finishing stitches will cover over some of the stitching, but on a dark-colored fabric, white or ivory stitching really stands out. The markers make the process go faster. Find permanent color markers in a rainbow of bright and standard colors at your local office supply store.*

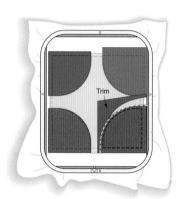

22. Repeat step 10 (trim close to the stitching).

23. Change the needle to a 90/14, change the thread to a 30-weight and slow the machine speed to embroider the decorative stitching.

24. Return the hoop to the machine and finish with decorative stitching, changing thread colors to match each fabric color.

25. Stitch segment 7 (perimeter stitching near seam allowance) while using your fingers to hold the fabrics in place as the machine stitches over the layers. After the perimeter stitching is finished, your block is complete.

26. Turn the block to the wrong side and trim on the outermost stitching line (3½" perimeter square).

27. Repeat steps 1 through 26 three or more times to develop the overall design, as shown above. Try combining the design with solid embroidered blocks for creative interest.

Designs that can be used for this technique:

Corner Circles

Crooked Squares

Wheel

Wheeling Around

The Wheel design combines the basic piecing techniques with the applipiecing technique to create a fun rotation of color. It takes four hoopings to create a complete wheel. The instructions below are for embroidery machine piecing.

For sewing machine piecing, follow the steps found in Chapter 2, pages 15 through 17, substituting the Wheel for the Triangle Border. Use sewing machine decorative stitches to finish the raw edges.

Note: Instructions are for using a cut-away stabilizer as the foundation.

1. Load the Wheel design onto the touch-screen of your embroidery machine.

2. Hoop the stabilizer.

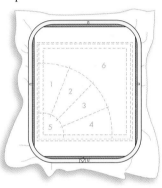

3. Stitch the entire design except for the decorative stitching without fabric. Turn off the machine "stops," if your machine has this feature, but don't forget to turn the "stops" back on after this step. Watch the design stitch to identify the steps for fabric placement. Stop the machine before the decorative segments stitch.

4. Remove the hoop from the machine and cut a piece of fabric large enough to cover the section 1. Be generous with your fabric cutting. Be sure the fabric extends beyond the section perimeter stitching lines.

5. Place the fabric over the area, return the hoop to the machine and stitch segment 2.

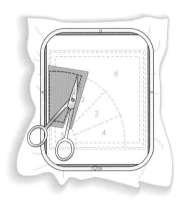

6. Remove the hoop from the machine; do not unhoop the fabric. Trim the excess fabric away from the stitching lines between sections 1 and 2.

7. Cut a piece of fabric large enough to cover section 2 plus the seam allowances.

8. Place the fabric over the stitching line between sections 1 and 2.

9. Return the hoop to the machine and stitch segment 3.

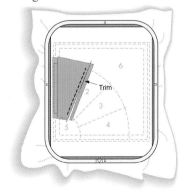

10. Remove the hoop from the machine and trim close to the stitching.

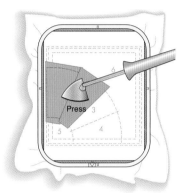

11. Place on an ironing surface and press the fabric open toward section 2.

12. Cut a piece of fabric large enough to cover section 3 plus the seam allowances.

13. Place the fabric over the stitching line between sections 2 and 3.

14. Return the hoop to the machine and stitch segment 4.

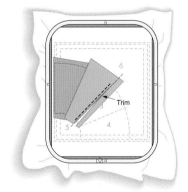

15. Remove the hoop from the machine and trim close to the stitching.

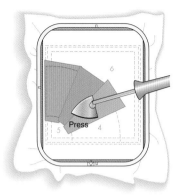

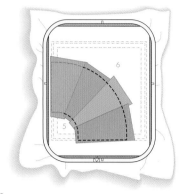

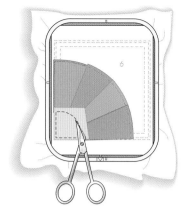

16. Place on an ironing surface and press the fabric open toward section 3.

17. Cut a piece of fabric large enough to cover section 4 plus the seam allowances.

18. Place the fabric over the stitching line between sections 3 and 4.

19. Return the hoop to the machine and stitch segment 5.

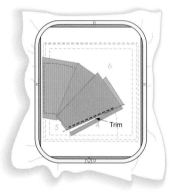

20. Remove the hoop from the machine and trim close to the stitching.

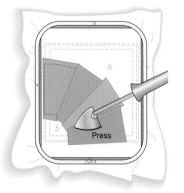

21. Place on an ironing surface and press the fabric open toward section 4.

22. Stitch segment 6 (perimeter stitching near seam allowance) while using your fingers to hold the fabric in place as the machine stitches over the layers.

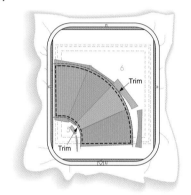

23. Trim the excess fabric from sections 1 through 4 that are inside sections 5 and 6.

24. Cut a piece of fabric large enough to cover section 5 plus the seam allowances. Be sure the fabric extends beyond the outermost block cutting line.

25. Place the fabric over section 5.

26. Return the hoop to the machine, change the needle to a 14/90, change the thread to a 30-weight color that matches the fabric and stitch segment 7.

27. Remove the hoop from the machine and trim close to the stitching.

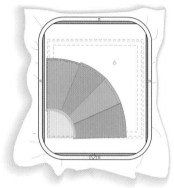

28. Slow the machine speed and embroider segment 8, which becomes the decorative stitching that covers the fabric raw edge.

29. Cut a piece of fabric large enough to cover section 6 plus the seam allowances. Be sure the fabric extends beyond the outermost block cutting line.

30. Place the fabric over section 6.

31. Return the hoop to the machine, change the thread to a 30-weight color that matches the fabric and stitch segment 9.

Jeanine recommends: Slowing the machine speed when using decorative stitching and a heavier-weight thread allows all the machine components to embroider smoothly and accurately. The thread has enough time to lay smoothly onto the fabric surface, providing a well-balanced stitch. Be sure to use a larger-eye needle with a heavier-weight thread.

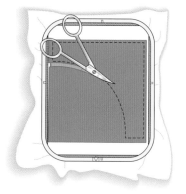 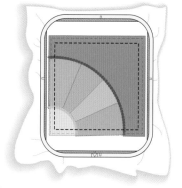 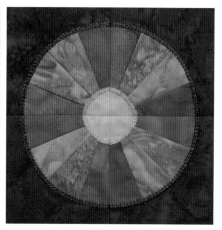

32. Remove the hoop from the machine and trim close to the stitching.

33. Slow the machine speed and embroider segment 10, which becomes the decorative stitching that covers the fabric raw edge.

34. Change the thread to a 40-weight and stitch segment 11 (perimeter stitching near seam allowance) while using your fingers to hold the fabrics in place as the machine stitches over the layers. After the perimeter stitching is finished, your block is complete.

35. Turn the block to the wrong side and trim on the outermost stitching line (3½" perimeter square).

36. Repeat this process three more times to complete the wheel block, as shown above.

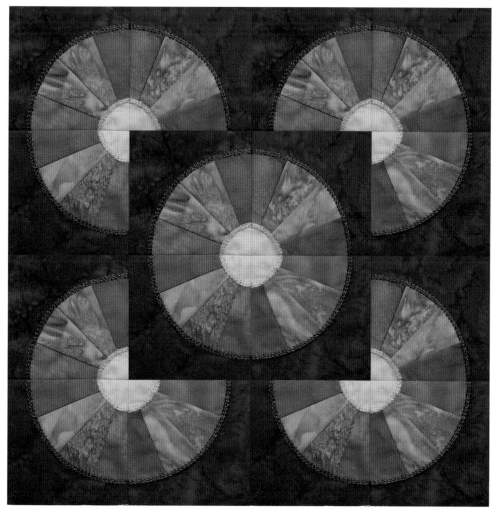

Use a complete wheel block with surrounding partial blocks to create an eye-catching combination for a wall hanging.

CHAPTER 6

Creative Piecing

The doll project is the ultimate combination of all the piecing techniques, plus some charming hand-sewn details. You'll have fun making her special. Make a quilt and use the leftover fabric to create a framed angel to coordinate. The wings are a separate design file and embroidered dimensionally using layers of sparkle organza. Complete step-by-step instructions can be found on the CD included on the inside back cover of this book.

Creative Piecing Basics

Creative piecing combines an assortment of piecing techniques with decorative embroidery machine stitches.

Step-by-Step Instructions

This clever purse is a great pattern or design for learning this technique, with the instructions below given for using your embroidery machine.

For sewing machine piecing, follow the steps found in Chapter 2, pages 15 through 17, substituting the Purse pattern for the Triangle Border pattern. Use sewing machine decorative stitches to finish the raw edges and to create a handle.

Note: Instructions are for using a cut-away stabilizer as the foundation.

1. Open the Purse design onto the touch-screen of your embroidery machine.

2. Hoop the stabilizer.

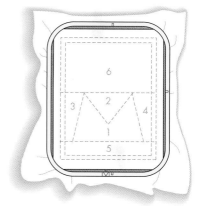

3. Stitch the entire design except for the decorative stitching without fabric. Turn off the machine "stops," if your machine has this feature, but don't forget to turn the "stops" back on after this step. Watch the design stitch to identify the steps for fabric placement. Stop the machine before the decorative segments stitch.

4. Remove the hoop from the machine and cut a piece of fabric large enough to cover section 1. Be generous with your fabric cutting. Be sure the fabric extends beyond the section perimeter stitching lines.

5. Place the fabric over the area, return the hoop to the machine and stitch segment 2.

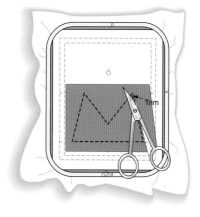

6. Remove the hoop from the machine and trim the excess fabric away from the stitching lines on all sides.

7. Cut a piece of fabric large enough to cover section 2 and place the fabric over section 2.

8. Return the hoop to the machine, change the thread color to match the fabric or use clear monofilament thread if desired and stitch segment 3.

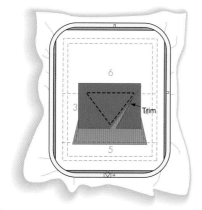

9. Remove the hoop from the machine and trim close to the stitching line on all sides.

10. Cut a piece of fabric large enough to cover section 3.

11. Place the fabric over the stitching line between sections 1 and 3.

12. Return the hoop to the machine and stitch segment 4.

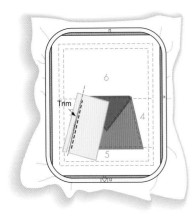

13. Remove the hoop from the machine and trim close to the stitching.

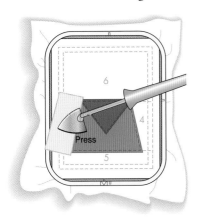

14. Place on an ironing surface and press the fabric open toward section 3.

15. Cut a piece of fabric large enough to cover section 4 plus the seam allowances. Be sure the fabric extends beyond the outermost block cutting line.

16. Place the fabric over the stitching line between sections 1 and 4.

17. Return the hoop to the machine and stitch segment 5.

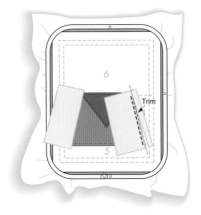

18. Remove the hoop from the machine and trim close to the stitching.

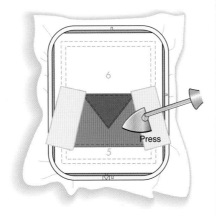

19. Place on an ironing surface and press the fabric open toward section 4.

20. Cut a piece of fabric large enough to cover section 5.

21. Place the fabric over the stitching line between sections 1, 3 and 4.

22. Return the hoop to the machine and stitch segment 6.

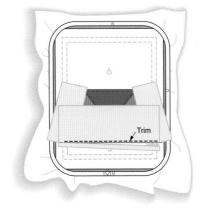

23. Remove the hoop from the machine and trim close to the stitching.

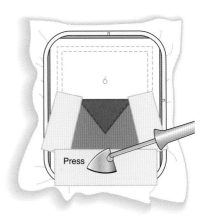

24. Place on an ironing surface and press the fabric open toward section 5.

25. Cut a piece of fabric large enough to cover section 6.

26. Place the fabric over the stitching line between sections 1, 3 and 4.

27. Return the hoop to the machine and stitch segment 7.

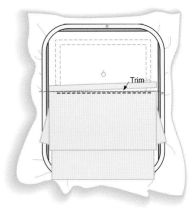

28. Remove the hoop from the machine and trim close to the stitching.

29. Place on an ironing surface and press the fabric open toward section 6.

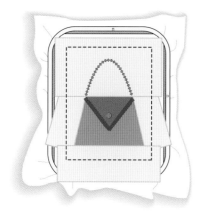

30. Stitch segment 8 (perimeter stitching near seam allowance) while using your fingers to hold the fabrics in place as the machine stitches over the layers.

31. Change the needle, depending on the thread weight, and change the thread to embroider segment 9 (the handle outline), segment 10 (the decorative stitching), segment 11 (the flap decorative stitching) and segment 12 (the closure). Slow the machine speed. Segment 11 is digitized to be embroidered with 30-weight thread. The handle and purse can be embroidered in all one thread color or changed at each color stop. After the decorative stitching is finished, your block is complete.

32. Remove the fabric from the hoop. Turn to the stabilizer side of the block and trim directly on the outermost stitching line (4" x 5" perimeter).

CREATIVE OPTION:

For the look shown in the photo at the right, hand-sew beads directly over segment 9 (the handle outline) instead of embroidering segment 10 (the handle).

Hand-sew a button onto the purse flap instead of embroidering segment 12 (the closure).

Designs that can be used for this technique:

Coffee Cup

Doll

Purse

Vintage Piecing

Add a vintage look to pieced projects by using a cut-away water-soluble foundation and unwashed flannel. Here's how:

1. Hoop a layer of cut-away water-soluble stabilizer.

2. Cut a piece of unwashed flannel the size of the inner hoop.

3. Complete the embroidery process as mentioned in Chapter 3, starting on page 18.

4. Use another layer of flannel as the batting and a backing layer. Stitch in the seam ditches with cotton thread or quilt the layers together using one of the designs on the CD.

5. Wash and dry the fabric layers in a mesh laundry bag or zippered pillowcase before using the piece in a project. The cut-away water-soluble stabilizer will have been removed, making way for vintage pieces that look like they are from long ago.

Before and after.

Pieced Appliqué

Using a pieced block for an appliqué design can yield successful results. When using a larger border design, it is possible to get multiple appliqués from one pieced block.

Refer to the Bulletin Board project on the CD for step-by-step appliqué instructions. There are also several appliqué designs featured on the CD included with this book.

Piecing with Batting

Add a thin layer of batting between the foundation and the fabric pieces to create blocks with loft. This technique is particularly great with embroidery machine piecing. Use a cut-away stabilizer and a low-loft polyester batting. Here's how:

1. Hoop the cut-away stabilizer.

2. Cut a piece of low-loft polyester batting the inner hoop size.

3. Place the batting on top of the stabilizer and complete the embroidery process as mentioned in Chapter 3, starting on page 18. Since the end result is a little added fluff to the blocks, this technique may eliminate the need for added batting for projects after the blocks are seamed together.

4. A backing is still required; stitch the backing to the blocks in the seamline ditches with monofilament thread instead.

Stained Glass

A pattern or design that includes thin black fabric between segment sections is considered a stained glass effect in piecing. The thin black fabric sections represent the "lead." The use of batik fabrics for the larger fabric sections represents the "glass" for this technique.

The same look can be achieved with any pattern or design by fusing bias binding after stitching segment seams and before adding the next fabric layer.

1. Use a craft iron to press the fabric toward the appropriately numbered section after stitching a seam (starting with segment 3 for embroidery machine piecing).

2. Cut a piece of ¼" fusible bias binding the fabric length that was just seamed to the foundation.

3. Fuse the binding to the fabric.

4. Continue steps 1 through 3 until the block is complete. Do not unhoop the fabric for embroidery machine piecing.

5. Use a sewing machine to stitch the bias binding in place with a 3.0 double needle and thread to match the bias binding. In some cases, it will be necessary to start sewing near the center, starting and stopping for each section.

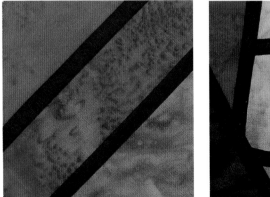

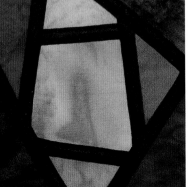

Segment Elimination

Pieced blocks do not need to be sewn or embroidered in their entirety. It is possible to forward past seamlines to eliminate fabric sections. For example, the Pineapple block can be started at segment 7 or segment 11, eliminating the smaller block sections.

Refer to the Design Details, starting on page 43, to determine which designs can be altered to create new blocks.

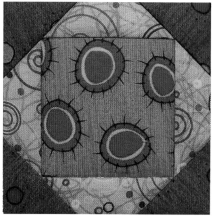

Pineapple design segments 11 through 18.

Piecing Experiments

Once all the concepts of piecing have been explored take it one step further to experiment with other fabrics and materials—from fleece to paper.

◀ PIECING WITH FLEECE

Use a thin microfiber fleece and a design with larger pieces. The seams tend to get a little bulky; be sure to use a cut-away stabilizer and trim the seam allowances close. This will reduce the buildup of seam allowances and make the process easier.

Use a small quilting design to hold the layers together. A water-soluble topping will keep the stitches from sinking in, or embroider the quilting design twice for a more prominent effect.

PIECING WITH SILK

The use of silk dupioni can offer a hint of elegance to piecing. The fabric is lightweight, has a sheen and provides texture to the finished block.

Use an assortment of bright colors to showcase brilliant color within a project.

Keep in mind that most silk dupioni is dry clean only. Use it in projects that will not be washed. ▶

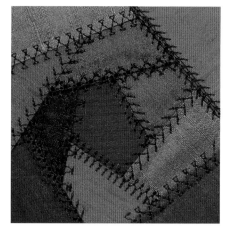

PIECING WITH PAPER

Try piecing with paper for framed cards and quilting scrapbook pages.

Use a cut-away stabilizer and handmade paper, as it has just the right consistency for piecing.

After stitching the seamline, fold the paper back gently. For a smooth seam fold, crease the paper back just before the seamline. Handle paper gently since it tears easily. ▼

EMBROIDER, THEN PIECE

Embroider the fabric first before using it in piecing projects.

Use a water-soluble stabilizer when embroidering the fabric and then soak to remove the stabilizer. Allow the fabric to dry and press the fabric from the wrong side.

The added stitching of the fabric enhances the overall appearance of the block. Bonus quilting designs are available on the CD included with this book. ▶

HAND-SEWN CHARM

The addition of beads, baubles, buttons and charms to piecing can make a project unique. Personalizing blocks with hand-sewn stitches along with an assortment of trinkets found at a specialty craft store can add pizzazz to any piecing project. ▶

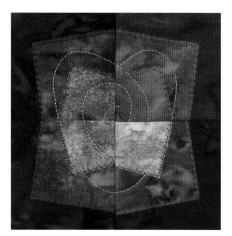

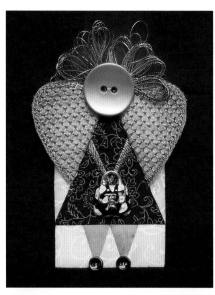

BLACK-AND-WHITE PIECING

A variety of black-and-white prints add a dramatic element to piecing. Several of the designs on the CD have areas for small embroidery designs.

Add block interest with one of the several bonus quilting designs available on the CD.

Piece the block and then embroider the design in the center of the starting section. The designs have been sized to fit perfectly with the piecing designs. ▶

Quilting Layers

The CD has an assortment of bonus quilting designs that can be used during or after the block construction to hold block, batting and backing layers together.

To quilt layers, hoop the pieced top, batting and batting layers together and embroider the quilting design.

Use a 30-weight cotton embroidery thread in the needle with a standard bobbin thread to match the backing. If the bobbin thread is not available in the backing fabric color, use a 60-weight cotton embroidery thread to match in the bobbin.

Border Piecing

Use the border designs for appliqué pieces, fabric segments for another pieced project, or as a border for a quilt project. The borders can be used whole or cut in half lengthwise and sewn end-to-end to get more mileage from one hooping.

For best results, do not try to miter the border corners. Use the borders along the straight edges. Sew side edges first, and then stitch the upper and lower edges.

Bind the raw edges using your favorite method.

Projects on the CD

Step-by-step instructions for these 12 projects can be found on the CD attached to this book's back cover.

Project 1: All Dolled Up

Project 2: Badge Holder

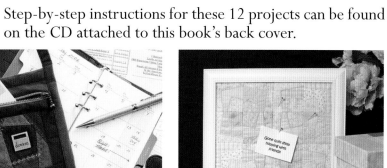

Project 3: Bulletin Board

Project 4: Coffee Gift Bag

Project 5: Crazy Patch Purse

Project 6: Framework

Project 7: Gentleman's Box

Project 8: Pamper Bucket

Project 9: Pieced Appliqué Sweatshirt

Project 10: Pincushion

Project 11: Reversible Piecework

Project 12: Table Tray

Resources

Look for these and other embroidery products at a local retailer where embroidery machines, software and designs are sold. To find a dealer near you, contact these companies of interest.

Fabrics

Visit your local quilt fabric shop for fat-eighths, fat-quarters or die-cut square samplers that are perfect for embroidery and sewing machine foundation piecing.

Fat Quarter Shop
(866) 826-2069
www.fatquartershop.com

Keepsake Quilting
(800) 865-9458
www.keepsakequilting.com

Nancy's Notions
(800) 833-0690
www.nancysnotions.com

Embroidery Publications
Creative Machine Embroidery
(800) 677-5212
www.cmemag.com

Designs in Machine Embroidery
(888) SEW-0555
www.dzgns.com

Embroidery Journal
(480) 419-0167
www.embroideryjournal.com

Embroidery Machine Companies
Baby Lock
(800) 422-2952
www.babylock.com

Bernina
(800) 405-2739
www.berninausa.com

Brother
(800) 422-7684
www.brother.com

Elna
(800) 848-3562
www.elnausa.com

Viking Sewing Machines
(800) 358-0001
www.husqvarnaviking.com

Janome
(800) 631-0183
www.janome.com

Kenmore
(888) 809-7158
www.sears.com

Pfaff
(800) 997-3233
www.pfaff.com

Simplicity
(800) 553-5332
www.simplicitysewing.com

Singer
(800) 474-6437
www.singershop.com

White
(800) 311-3164
www.whitesewing.com

Design Details

Coffee Cup (Cup)

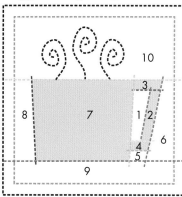

Size: 3.50" x 3.50" (88.9mm x 88.9mm)
Starting piece: 1" x 1.25"
Cut strips: .75" and 1.5", Piece 6: 2.25" square,
Piece 10: 2" x 4"

Corner Circles (Circles)

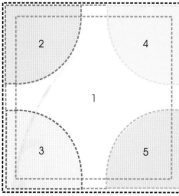

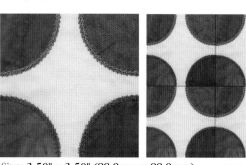

Size: 3.50" x 3.50" (88.9mm x 88.9mm)
Starting piece: 4" square
Cut strips: 1.75"

Tip: Great for scraps!

Crazy Log Cabin (CLCabin)

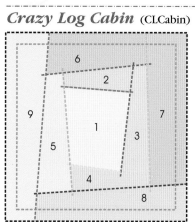

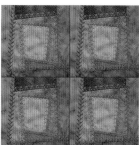

Size: 3.50" x 3.50" (88.9mm x 88.9mm)
Starting piece: 1.75" square
Cut strips: 1.25"

Crazy Patch 1 (CPatch1)

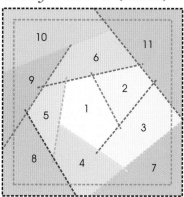

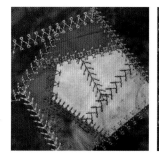

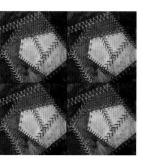

Size: 3.50" x 3.50" (88.9mm x 88.9mm)
Starting piece: 1.75" square
Cut strips: 1.75"

Crazy Patch 2 (CPatch2)

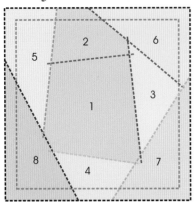

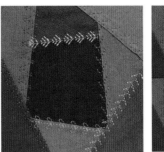

Size: 3.50" x 3.50" (88.9mm x 88.9mm)
Starting piece: 2.5" square
Cut strips: 1.75"

Crooked Log Cabin (LogCabin)

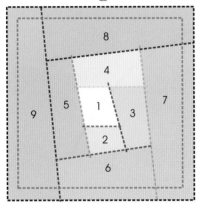

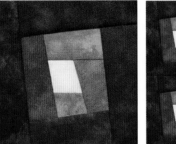

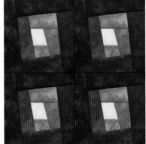

Size: 3.50" x 3.50" (88.9mm x 88.9mm)
Starting piece: 1"
Cut strips: 1" (1, 2, 3, 4, 5) and 1.5" (6, 7, 8, 9)

Crooked Squares (Squares)

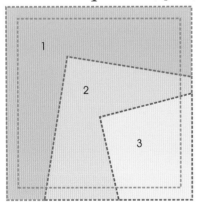

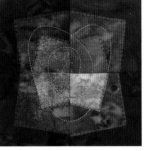

Size: 3.50" x 3.50" (88.9mm x 88.9mm)
Starting piece: 4" square
Piece 2: 3" square, Piece 3: 2" square

Diamond Center (DiamCntr)

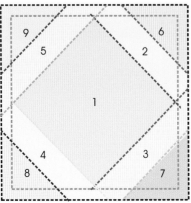

Size: 3.50" x 3.50" (88.9mm x 88.9mm)
Starting piece: 3.5" square
Cut strips: .75" (2, 3, 4, 5) and 1.25" (6, 7, 8, 9)

Doll (Doll)

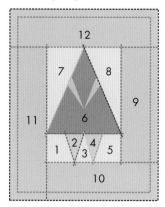

Size: 4" x 5" (101.6mm x 127.5mm)
Starting piece: 1" square
Cut strips: 1.5"   Piece 6: 2.5" x 3"

Heart (Heart)

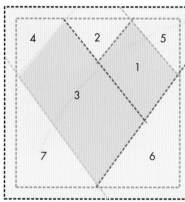

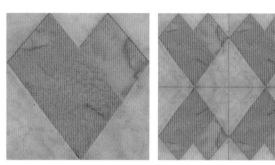

Size: 3.50" x 3.50" (88.9mm x 88.9mm)
Starting piece: 1.5" square
Cut strips: 2"   Piece 3: 2" x 3"

Pineapple (Pineaple)

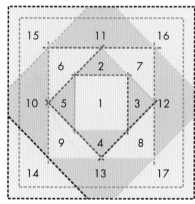

Size: 3.50" x 3.50" (88.9mm x 88.9mm)
Starting piece: 1.25" square
Cut strips: 1" and 1.5" (14, 15, 16, 17)

Tip:Great for scraps!

Purse (Purse)

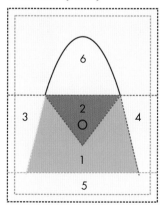

Size: 4" x 5" (101.6mm x 127.5mm)
Starting piece: 2.25" x 3.35"
Cut strips: 1.5" square, Piece 2: 1.75" x 2.5", Piece 6: 2.5" x 4"

Stained Glass (StainGl)

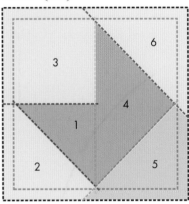

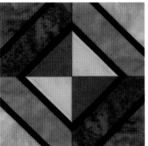

Size: 4" x 5" (101.6mm x 127.5mm)
Starting piece: 1.5" x 5"
Cut strips: 2" (or use 3.375" squares cut in half on the diagonal to make two triangles.   Black strips: .75"

Star (Star)

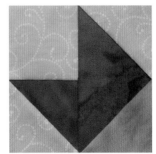

Size: 3.50" x 3.50" (88.9mm x 88.9mm)
Starting piece: 1.5" x 2.5"
Cut strips: 2"

Stripe Border (StriBrdr)

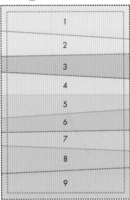

Size: 4.50" x 6.50" (114.3mm x 165.1mm)
Starting piece: 1.5" x 5"
Cut strips: 1.5" x 5"

Tip: Pre-cut strip pieces

Triangle Border (TriBrdr)

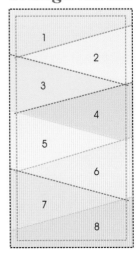

Size: 3.50" x 6.50"
(88.9mm x 165.1mm)
Starting piece: 2" x 4.5"
Cut strips: 2" x 4.5"

Tip: Pre-cut strip pieces

Triangle Log Cabin (TriLogCb)

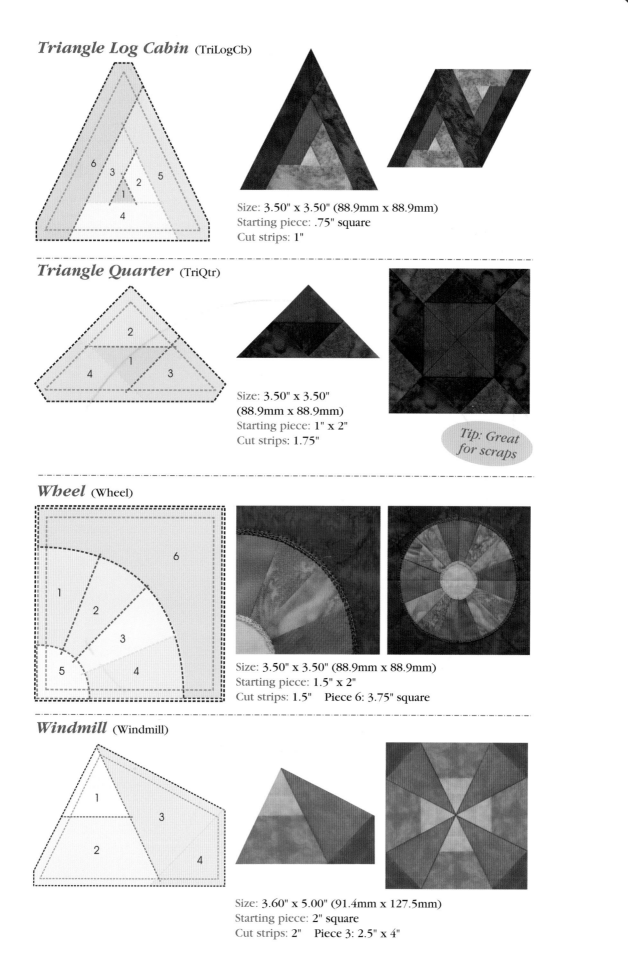

Size: 3.50" x 3.50" (88.9mm x 88.9mm)
Starting piece: .75" square
Cut strips: 1"

Triangle Quarter (TriQtr)

Size: 3.50" x 3.50"
(88.9mm x 88.9mm)
Starting piece: 1" x 2"
Cut strips: 1.75"

Tip: Great for scraps

Wheel (Wheel)

Size: 3.50" x 3.50" (88.9mm x 88.9mm)
Starting piece: 1.5" x 2"
Cut strips: 1.5"   Piece 6: 3.75" square

Windmill (Windmill)

Size: 3.60" x 5.00" (91.4mm x 127.5mm)
Starting piece: 2" square
Cut strips: 2"   Piece 3: 2.5" x 4"

47

For more information on embroidery, purchase additional titles in this series: Embroidery Machine Essentials; More Embroidery Machine Essentials; Companion Project Series Book 1: Basic Techniques; Companion Project Series Book 2: Fleece Techniques; Companion Project Series Book 3: Quilting Techniques; and Companion Project Series Book 4: Appliqué Techniques.

CD Instructions

The embroidery designs featured in this book are located on the CD. You must have a computer and compatible embroidery software to access and utilize the decorative designs. Basic computer knowledge is helpful to understand how to copy the designs onto the hard drive of your computer.

To access the designs, insert the CD into your computer. The designs are located on the CD in folders for each embroidery machine format. Copy the design files onto the computer hard drive using one of the operating system (Windows) programs or open the design in applicable embroidery software. Be sure to copy only the design format compatible with your brand of embroidery equipment.

Once the designs are in your embroidery software or saved on your computer, transfer the designs to your embroidery machine following the manufacturer's instructions for your equipment. For more information about using these designs with your software or embroidery equipment, consult your owner's manual or seek advice from the dealer who honors your equipment warranty.